REALITY WAYFARERS

Linda King

Reality Wayfarers by Linda King is published and printed in the USA by Shoe Music Press, Alpharetta, GA. ©2014 Shoe Music Press and Linda King. All Rights Reserved.

Cover Image *Grand Central* by Sally Gooding. ©2014 Sally Gooding.

ISBN-13: 978-0692271735

ISBN-10: 0692271732

Also by Linda King : *Dream Street Details*

For Ellie

CONTENTS

all you possess is metaphor

paths plus centre	1
notes	2
this world is always sorry	3
highways and being	4
no truth in time	5
everything shines by reflection	6
still life	7
undersong	8
exhausted of possibility	9
you hear all the dark violins	11
all you possess is metaphor	13
pattern recognition	14
cipher	15
not to scale	16
last bastion of illusion	17
the truth approximate	18
shadow maker	19
late to heal	20
existential implications	21

reality wayfarers

the verb exist is not a real predicate	25
diffraction	26
only light remembers its origins	27
common accidentals	28
waiting room	29
any kind of magic	30
cocktail hour	32
reality wayfarers	33
codeine dreams	34
act one	35
every inked-in person	36
on the coast of forgiveness	37
path of least resistance	38
a latecomer to reality	39
cut and paste existentialism	40

the pivot point   41
therapeutic range   42
elements inhabit you   43
damage done   44
this tangle of things   45

shadows prove the light

that double pull   49
stones will weigh you down   50
subtle truths detected   51
a lifespan is a billion heartbeats   53
dissolve   55
oxygen   56
the actor's point of view   57
only one cure   58
aftershocks   59
naming   60
shadows prove the light   61
witness   62

Acknowledgements   64

Author Bio   65

all you possess is metaphor

paths plus centre

you need hunger to be duped by reality
the always dream passes between
carries across the metaphor
that breathing is all one breath
what is it if not forever?

the storyline cracks open
into childhood questions we all live with
each night's wreckage moves into the day's fiction
all of it thrown down on paper
shabby tricks

house with all white rooms
you crawl through them
on a midsummer day
a pilgrim in the labyrinth at Chartres
where no logic goes clear

definitions will disappoint you
all that real stuff on the sidelines
the infinity ledge   bits of your life
some plausible version of truth
the way that fallen leaves prove the wind

notes

shadow world
everything an approximation

mistakes
about time and date

philosophic
blur of elsewhere

the only promise
a lure

listen
and listen again

there should be music
a returning home

spaces
in that hangman's game

a world balanced
above nothingness

the ever living fire
made flesh and blood

beating hearts
asleep in the burning house

this world is always sorry

what you are moving toward   unfurling
universe of pure randomness
differing modes of fundamental anxiety
cause sui   the space between

each imperative forms tiny patterns
with no correlation between
the thing and the naming

this world is always sorry
for what is wanting
it speaks mean truths
in threatening weather
leaves you in the dark
covered with voices
from the being thieves

that trap of language
everything a metaphor
like the quality of lamplight
stones you swallow   glass shattering

you left home
heading in the wrong direction

disinherit the pearls
it is your notion of reality
that is tied with knotted string

what you get for existing
is a little heartbreaking kindness
and those twenty-six letters

highways and being

devoid of reason   chance corners you
in some altered place
that is just metaphor

there are too many names for being
this universe is indifferent
to all of them

beyond and behind
what you believe
between the actual and the real

on the edge of language
there is no solution
nothing left

the emptiness gathers
devours
all the hours

those walls dream of you
it's another way to disappear
like small print fading

all of it
a useless attempt
to unhurt yourself

no truth in time

and yet there are first things
green at every window
the sound of five hundred horses running
the loyalty of a camera's lens
or the soft light you find
in a one-windowed room

the philosophers confide in you
they speak the language of maps
mistaken dialogues

all of it
a far-flung metaphor *metafora*
metaferin   meta (across)
                                            ferin (to carry)

temptress or muse
reality is coercion

like that red cape
worn into the woods
or a taste of just right porridge

                            it is not time
                            it is never time
for an appeal to blood

you watch the clock parts spill out
take only what you can hold
in your hands

everything shines by reflection

      we all seek clemency
aftermath of rust and blood
relationality is what counts

            all that is perceptually available
                is revealed to be loss
                    causes begun
                  before existence

silent dialogue   clear-cut truth
none of this moves towards meaning
it just folds you into some other time

still life

you want to become
an ordinary afternoon

coax the magic
from reason's predicament

it's a question
of folding and unfolding

that
slippery Heideggerian argument

a distantiation
of distance

simulacrum
is your grateful landscape

all the edges
gone fluid

here   settle
stay awhile

sleep   the sleep of the cat
curled around your hair

undersong

the existential tower
leans slightly to the left
toward meaning   toward
some dimension of reality
various latitudes
all that lonely water

turn up the treble
the language mystic
wants to name something

you were promised nothing
but a thought-up real world
of things and objects

evidence is withheld
there is a quiet weeping
a sort of madness
everywhere a dialect of loss
another narrative
forest lost to flames

the wolves are howling again
you wonder if they measure time by night
this is no small thing in the space of now

displaced logic without form will freefloat
it is always the background music
that you take to be real

exhausted of possibility

mark the damaged areas
note the exit signs
shake out being's wet garments

there is no temporal order
the threat of meaninglessness
is everywhere

reality is filtered
through the illustrations
of this world

your own projections
of the possible
stretch the black night

a night
when language sleeps
in an abandoned house

every room
an absolute space
of grief

someone offers up
the unnecessary
confession

but you know that a river
is not the meaning
of a river

and
like a bell
waiting to be struck

you
can never arrive
at the beginning of things

you hear all the dark violins

in some small language that names you
is a pull stronger than gravity
or undertow

words arranged to look true

strike the red match   steal fire from the gods
the navigators are at the centre of the void

you are up against
a procession of lonely roads
and your wild hands frame the moon

you keep on   counting things
collect rulers   measuring cups   musical notes

reality is mostly nouns
like the discrete mystic
or the myth of knowing

common discourse dictates metaphor's reflection
old dreams are true for a long time
a stance toward reality
cart before the horse

the trick is to admit to everything
pockets full of blood
inflatable life jackets under the seat

skirt all the checkpoints
rub your name into each paragraph
let them believe in cause and effect
everyone hides in the wreckage

while you circle spin
in the middle of the freeway

all you possess is metaphor

an understanding of light

                night's music shadows

every grace
that doesn't fade
by morning

                                small islands

                                        of the real

      dark smudges from dead fires

tower of rubble
tower of babble

no story is simple

                today's reality is handheld

                        a little blood seeping out

every phone call
a demand for money

                send packages and letters

those scattered things
guilty of nothing

pattern recognition

you anticipate calamity   on the edge of chaos

you make what you see answer your questions

your mind composes you   stitches the ragged edges

attempts to mend holes in the fabric of the real

there is only one here   and only one else (w) here

like an answer that didn't exist before

everything is subject to the random

or an odd combination of pharmaceuticals

hit the properties key

there are three of you on the page

with no camouflage

pay attention

everything   is   every   thing

                                          a state of grace
                                        the space between
                                      an elaborate illusion

...an error message

cipher

all landmarks overflow their points of reference
like that map of London where you circle marble arch
a confused matrix of starting points
map folded into various realms of reality

such pretty references grasp nothing
but the shape of memory

muttering   muttering
along the corridor   then up the stairs

you keep thinking there is something missing
look for a way to implicate the scavengers
you know that nothing will stem the bleeding

philosophy is broken
there is no meeting place
for the truth searchers

like rust or moss
or seashells inked with black
there is no chance to show mercy
everything is already something else

not to scale

how god-like
this naming
of things

truth
neither presence
nor absence

but the in-between difference
that translates
to sameness

particles
arranged
around beingness

the site
of memory   maps
a language

doctored photographs
are full time witnesses
to illusion

to
the soft eyes
of believers

or the way
that everyone looks smaller
on the horizon

last bastion of illusion

traces you leave

                    footprints
                    fingerprints
                    flakes of skin

survive into text
barbed-wire words
someone else's script
the always rehearsal

you clothe yourself
in disguise

you will not apologize

skeleton of memory
the final brushstrokes

                    language
                    the body ignores

truths
were always there

full of all that
and nothing

bell curving
roll of two dice

                    another clue
                    snapping at your heels

the truth approximate

blame god for not existing   being bears too heavy a load

for such a narrow path   learn to read and speak in the dark

find your notes on the transcendental turn

add some measure of reason   an image that bends

a slight miscalculation

every morning you face the dilemma   what to do

with leftover dreams   add another chemical to the mix

gather the light   what lives is small

and hungry for what has not been tasted

shadow maker

essence reaches   over language

that roaring inside you   the truth of your mouth

a world of mythmaking given over to some kind of reality

                                               a seaming of threads

they have made a church of you

and the way you rewrite their stories

                                       through the fire
                                       diffused sunlight
                                       puppet showmen

we are all prisoners in a world of shadow

chip away enough of the cave wall and you are left with nothing

                             blank stare   blank page   blank wall

                                                   blanketyblankblank

nothing outside this witness
but a brief stuttering life

late to heal

philosophers are moving targets
Kierkegaard broke his own heart
all that desperately addressing the plausible
hovering over the truth

the language of all things
remains outside the text   ruptured reality
leap over oblivion   a folder
with everyone's name on it

formal procedures are required
arrange the ideas for today
you are not responsible
for compromised realities
or the impossible past
some scars are late to heal

language's fluid boundaries
are a way to understand the unknown
existence as erasure   this blank page
the ordinary ironic fairytale quest

all inherited meanings
wait on the street corners
for something to be true

existential implications

the essence of reason
equals nothing but the memory of words
pattern of dust   french paper   silk cuts
champagne glasses   nightlonging
philosophy on the menu

so much of what is real
is just a spelling mistake

and yet   your eyes follow
the lines on the paper

you will always need rescuing
there are too many proper names
alphabet signs   descending myths
all those temporary gods on the shelves

naming will not make it real
but you are the words
that everyone is compelled to write

reality wayfarers

the verb exist is not a real predicate

           we live in language
one sad fiction after another
a history that fits a pamphlet

stop looking for the real story
you need a richer vocabulary
not that stockpile of facts

sentences will betray you
internal duplicates
can differ

reality
has never been
a reliable witness

you need
new words
for each occasion

like the sky that speaks
in birdwings   or the ambiguity
of memories

that familiar gravity
with no fixed address

diffraction

rooms of the moment
small appreciations
some version of time
the source of the error
no instant of knowing
understanding of form
an absence you carry
chance encounters
language slips away
your body gone under

things divided by twilight
pebbles in the lake
a beginning or a loss
your symptoms invisible
only black ink scratching
all alternate possibilities
loss   decoded   exiled
with the world's default state
beyond flesh and bone
where reality bleeds out

only light remembers its origins

what your blood recalls
accumulates above the fault line
the weight of reason
windsong of anger
the trees   softened by rain
will bend backward

check your identity card
we are all reality conduits
feel for a pulse
remember to press hard enough
between the world and the thing
the telling and the untelling

illusion is the general rule
distinction between things
a hiatus

like the light from distant stars
the present will never reach
this small square of paper

language dwells in itself
the truth affords no solution
you will continue to interpret
what you already know
and the starlings in your hair
will go on singing

common accidentals

this is not a song
every note has left you

music requires a counting
a different system of protective measures

the accidental
may be cancelled at any time

a little brokenness shows
unfolds into another reality

you go on indenting paragraphs
although each phrase means at least two things

like water under ice
a moment in a mirror

an idea that unfolds
in nonlinear time

the heart's four chambers
contain portions of reality

scratch away
the black matted backing

it's all too mystical
everyone wants to rewrite Plato

to let one thing be another
like the crows that lift off this page

waiting room

feathers on fire   wings clipped
amazed skeletons watching
each syllable bends toward meaning
toward what cannot be explained

sorry hurls you through time and space
to that crying dream   that simple nightmare
where there are symptoms of overexposure
heft of memory   a wayward quickening

time is cruel medicine
your childhood sky rains useless pennies
cliff note alibis   playground games

prepare a toast to Heidegger
reality is not an easy place
every invoice   past due
the water rising

there is no trail here
everyone you meet is drawn in pencil
their clothes ravel in thin fabric
a tiny seam opens   unshelters
this small place of being

any kind of magic

in two orders of reality

things are never as expected

the centre of being-there wavers

in the afterness of words

no matter the language

it's all translation   false memories

everyone resembles the one who commits the crime

bone-dug down in the wreckage left behind

stories taped to the wall

                                      a bit of radiance
                                      a game of chance
                                      tip the whiskey glass

even the temporary gods

won't remember you

but   oh how you will confess

deconstruct yourself   rotate the text

wake-up in the wrong house

find that ruined party dress

full of heart-beaten

free-falling

reason

cocktail hour

like barges let loose from their moorings
everything that has left you   that you have left
drifts past the vanishing point
past Aristotle's six elements of tragedy

who can say what truth means…

the dazzle of falling space
the shape of a key
that small ball under the shell

science explained by magic
or cracks in perception

once you learned how to unwrap words
you told the same story for years
the bird-scratch dirt of small towns
still in your fingernails

trapped in being's roundabout
or some stage trick of reality
the curtain goes up in flames
there is no reason for this
just the always strange constant forever
artfully splattered with blood

eventually
explanations desert everyone
place the rusted flowers in crystal
let the host take your arm   follow him
along the crow-shadowed path to the party

wash your body with wine

reality wayfarers

you know the story
how the narrative shifts
anticipates departure
like sealing wax
or the broken logic of punishment

the last train gone past   your tears
break towns into raindrop windows
turn up the music   lace can be so cruel
and summer is really over

listen   listen
this night is crying
strangers wait in an endless series of rooms
stalls in the flea market of being

reality is bound to nothing
but a chain-of-events history
everything is what you already know
handful of sand   a farewell in stages
or a cautionary tale

you wear an old dress
name tag pinned to the collar
your pocketbook is full of gold stars

crows follow the woman you used to be
they will steal anything small and shiny

codeine dreams

                                        like everyone else
        you are an actor   relying on science
reality do-it-yourself kits with four kinds of matter
other passwords and perimeters

                                things come to things
the tiniest fragment of any day contains the infinite

luminosity is a different language

                          stars wait to be born
some foreign tongue speaks in present tense
letters drown on the page

perhaps
you will dance   cause accidents
you do like to measure things
prepare the correct dosage

we all swallow poison   work our way through
reasonable negotiations   some version of the facts
a history that fits

                                a hanging length of rope

act one

the real is disappearing
through an excess of reality
the symbolic dimension of language
no longer applies

all the messages are in the margins
where ink becomes history

the taste of salt in your mouth
is an old language
          an anti-pain killer

you are a memory full of song
once   you sang your dolls to sleep
your childhood was always winter
the robbed heat
          so small a picture

and yet
there was a ballroom
with a little raised stage
where you practiced
the art of illusion
and called it happiness

every inked-in person

everyone
is missing part of the picture
like waves illegible in the rain
trees burning for poems
essential contradictions

did you warn everyone?
thinned blood is redder

the larger picture
is a prize you won
snowglobe reality bite
some great chain of being
that high-wire act of childhood
your mannequin mother

only the little gods
have that thin blue light
it lifts the moon

the language you speak
is full of runaway sentences
theories riddled with riddles

ding dong bell   the kitty's in the well

people at bus stops
every inked-in person
a malnourished version
of Lucky or Pozzo

on the coast of forgiveness

begin with this
a brainstorm of being
pouring salt on the alphabet
stopped clock on the highway overpass

however tragic
the truth is punishment
punctuation marks that dissolve
like syllables in the rain

look for the objects of this world
handles   buttons   pedals
latches   all small causes

there are rumours of a cure
your name in a child's collection
of lettered blocks
all nonsense words

you write
to make your life possible
live on the coast of forgiveness
where reality bends in two
all those words and phrases spilling out
crows pecking the dead

path of least resistance

you want a walled garden   a whole galaxy of otherwise

that space   beyond the protection of here and now

you want your own way to be

shopping lists for the thrift shop existential

clear plastic shower curtain of reality

running shoes flung over hydro wires

such cruel mathematics   dead letter messages

like claps of thunder   all the gods are done with us

not knowing is best

sign your name to it

return home transformed

become water

a latecomer to reality

you miss the signs

light through a prism

an offering of evidence

distant voices   photographs

gunpowder residue in the whiskey

queen of hearts in the safety deposit box

reality reshuffles

the concept of meaning

is a maelstrom of facticity

an illusion that corresponds

to a physics of facts

cut and paste existentialism

reality will never clear the wreckage
the not-yet-but-yet-to-be
free will disappoints you
infinite freedom arises out of nothing
a thing among things

the external today
your own stream of experience
fear of truth   shared words
without meaning

carry your basket of metaphors into the mystic
be set apart from this world   empty of content
of silence and sound

look both ways   choose and decide
flesh and blood
breath and bone

days are not the measure
or possible cure
of being

the pivot point

patterns dissolve

between things

                behind you

                        uncharted

                                  degrees

                                      of reality

night's half journey

the moon's hour of meaning

oversight of exile

your passport stamped by diviners

a common eternity

or some holy thing

therapeutic range

your words angle towards a lasting real
things are out of place

the woven cloth of language
lacks significance   is faulty to the core

fragile things with no sense of direction
no subject matter

your proof of existence
is in the mail

forced colour fields
at the being borders

everything borrowed
from the reality landscape

every confused message
disguised as real

perceptual information in ringtones
a future that carries the past forward

but never allows you
to see the whole picture

elements inhabit you

your past a constant horizon
the sometimes evidence
of essentialness
luck behind you   somewhere

what did knowledge get you
and what is it anyway?
some trembling admiration
that dwelling of yesterday
all those unloved children

take that bag of crumbs along
this is the neighbourhood of the uncertain
no mercy   ever
tomorrow is a cage-trained dog

it's all perception
warp in the glass   smudge of lines
you lose the moorings of reason
your questions unanswered

a translation is not forthcoming
intentional cruelty is written into everything
the past never ends   there is presence
in absence   the real as transitory
train wreck in slow motion   you were
the child who went away in the dark
and again   you wonder
how it would feel to be water

damage done

lean over   fall in
you are losing presence
something gone wrong
or just gone

everything
returns
to something

is anyone listening?

history unbuckles the safety belt

                         you want
                         a better sort of wondering
                         a simple impossibility

something
to ease your knowing

like Kierkegaard's inkstained fingers

this tangle of things

the eternal problem with images
the girl in the photo
this tangle of things
that is too real
or not real enough

a matter of balance
false hopes formed of objects

(being takes up only three lines in your dictionary)

open up
the existential care package   unwrap
the stolen apples from your childhood

(apply Nietzsche's doctrine of perspective)

stop prowling in the past
where the outside looks in on you

history dissolves
into vanished stories

that child on the back stoop   imagining
that a concept of nothingness
is still something

shadows prove the light

that double pull

you want to grab onto those long chains of reason

like evening birds heading home

through the meanness of time

you want a little magic on your side

beat of music   like the rhythm of thrombosis

you believe that empty space is something

and the secrets every house knows

will pretend a simple plot   backlit

by the light from other moons

you are a woman with fevers

you skate that small circle of ice in the field for hours

your truth is in encountering such simple things

the easy way that words open a wound

existence as a continual alert

an image's thingness   that double pull

of a truth that never arrives

stones will weigh you down

everything is evidence   reason solves nothing
shine a light   shine a light   texture to form

less than atoms   other random thoughts
found in formal clothes

Heidegger's theory of temporal
inauthenticity

love song to being   here
at point-blank range

symmetry of circles
concentric

what reaches toward meaning
opens like a gift

one version
of truth

two layers of discourse
will break your heart

empty
your pockets

subtle truths detected

in a move toward evening   toward the wind's voice
the between of co-existence
wants no privileged point of view

it's all desperate details
attempts to hide the relevant paradox
like those hands held out along fourth avenue

the limits of ordinary language
require borrowed meanings
from the other side of the horizon

knowing this trick is a good thing
but keep your clothes quiet
the notion of being is sewn into your hem

like someone drowning
or crossing the road
you are blind

with nothing to look at
but a blackness
that absorbs all light

leave your face
on the vanity
mourn in proper fashion

you no longer know
how to have a body
you are an oath taken

the ghostbride
who walks the graveyard
tossing flowers

a lifespan is a billion heartbeats

there is no truth to time
but you grow older

your heart beats darkly
imagines forever

it is your fear
that entertains endings

but reason will not be
overthrown so easily

language is all being
every text a rain of words

an everburning memory
of every sad utterance

which are facts
and which are shadows?

within
the parameters of naming

reality blurs
as naming retreats

ignore
those flash card nouns

speak yourself
into a new language

take
a momentary exit

become
light and sound again

dissolve

go ahead
hang your lies on the wall
put on some music   play yourself
everyone is an ancestor   littered with debris
and no fixed address

you try to remember
where you have hidden
that small deck of magic cards
universal truth   randomly arranged

against all reason   you are inside time
outside reality's shift of history
you are no stranger here
it doesn't matter what they call you

consult your counterfeit atlas
move in every direction
go back four spaces

that soft light comes from swallowed matches
a reality seen through the filter of made-up stories
for which you write the endings

there are no memories
it's all surfaces with no reflection
shards of glass   lipstick stained party tricks
where lists of epitaphs dissolve on the tongue

oxygen

you sleep on a blank piece of paper
your dreams write the chemical news
a diffused blueprint for being

you line up
for your daily dose
of space and time
fabricate   reconfigure
this world of in-between

your thoughts
can sense themselves
sniffing the air

the actor's point of view

evenings like this
some call them losses
sleeping in white noise
eyes to last light
this void
and nothing

facts
flutter to the ground
leaves to the wind

random dramas
destinies
desires

there is a memory
that won't fit any language

no one
behind the curtain

step out
from the wings
put on your robes of being

find the bus ticket
in your pocket

only one cure

the meaning of life
stacked in the outlet mall
those uncommon things
like a looking glass
that won't hold your image

this world
of places on a map
you are here   somewhere
between the actual
and the imaginary

five perfect solids
equate to fifty faces
spatial replication
at the cosmetics counter

a petal orchard
or halting steps to the real
to that broken child
with stories long finished

you don't tell them
anymore

drink the whiskey
solipsism is underrated

aftershocks

some things do not translate
words stand in for illusion
brass lamp   bitter coffee
spit out the small shells

everyone waits
for the shaking to begin
mystery gets replaced by logic
the dust and smoke
of opaque knowledge
waterfall of memory
caught in the facts
in the motion of blue
where nothing can be forgiven

everyone presents
their own mask

wind the clock back a bit
those little pieces of time
inhabit the past

the snarl and bite of meaning
is no recourse for truth
no honest alibi

just the sharp knife
of perpetual imperfection

naming

your blacksmoke childhood
soft mistakes   warning signs
ill fortune after the rain
four points of departure
every void a placeholder
for the possible

most journeys are unmappable
caught in categorical imperatives
that snag of meaning
like blood vines on the garden wall
elements and anti-elements
every river moving on to somewhere else

in the hours before survival
you can get used to solitude
your own dark night
this world erasing you
no chorus   no song

just a slow merging of two silences
some frantic code number
meanings rinsed in regret
that double-sided consciousness of being
what becomes through the saying of it

pull the fabric taught
hold your breath
repeat your name aloud

shadows prove the light

points of convergence
reduce to pure refraction
a thousand pieces of scattered glass
like childhood's gravel roads
all those unhappy homes   abandoned

everything suspended
between being and truth
where the smallest action
or the yearning of birds
alters the course of this world

voices on the telephone
two hands reaching
dilation of time
the limit beyond
what ends

run your fingers
along the periphery
every interpretation is full of holes
a kind of filigreed reason

wave that pale flag
compose a glossary of loss
whatever you catalogue
becomes a path to innocence
or an anguish that freefloats forever

witness

follow the script of shiny words

salt-wound promises

all that lost luxury

stealing present tense

standing still   you move

in every direction

no home but the body

you are a black and white photo

cardboard box in the antique shop

frameless   never more than a narrative

borrowed for the time being

every shade of black

contains a metaphor

the middle distance   or a circle

where the world becomes the space around it

a crossing-over that moves

toward no horizon

ACKNOWLEDGEMENTS

Grateful acknowledgement is made to the following literary journals in which some of these poems first appeared:

Contemporary Verse 2

E-Ratio

Letterbox

Room

Streetcakes

The Inflectionist Review

MadHat Lit

My heartfelt thanks to Gordon Purkis of Shoe Music Press for his guidance through this journey – as gentle critic, editor and friend.

I am much indebted to Tara Wohlberg and Colette Gagnon – friends and fellow poets – for their invaluable insight and suggestions during the writing process.

Special thanks go to artist Sally Gooding for the brilliant artwork that graces the cover.

Perpetual thanks to Brian, for everything.

Linda King has been published in numerous literary journals in Canada and internationally. She is the author of *Dream Street Details* (Shoe Music Press, 2013). She studied philosophy at The University of Winnipeg and is a graduate of The Writers' Studio at Simon Fraser University. Originally from Ontario, she now lives and writes near the beach in Vancouver, BC.

About the Cover Artist:

Sally Gooding is a Vancouver-based Photographer and Mixed Media Artist. Her work has been shown in Canada and The United States and is characterised by a dream-like quality. Sally draws her inspiration from travels across the globe. For further information please visit www.sasabdesigns.com.

www.ingramcontent.com/pod-product-compliance
Lightning Source LLC
Chambersburg PA
CBHW022124040426
42450CB00006B/836